T0400476

VAMPIRE
LIFE CYCLES

by Noah Leatherland

BEARPORT
PUBLISHING

Minneapolis, Minnesota

Credits
All images courtesy of Shutterstock.com. With thanks to Getty Images, Thinkstock Photo, and iStockphoto. Cover – KingJC, Sergio Photone, Here, Jakub Krechowicz, sociologas, wabeno. Recurring – Elizaveta Mironets, sociologas, wabeno. P1 – KingJC. P4–5 – madorf, Raggedstone. P6–7 – LedyX, Ysbrand Cosijn. P8–9 – Carlos Caetano, Margaret M Stewart. P10–11 – marinafrost, Rawpixel.com. P12–13 – FOTOKITA, PublicDomain/Wikimedia, Nathapol Kongseang, Gino Santa Maria. P14–15 – Kiselev Andrey Valerevich,Sandstein/Wikimedia, Digital Storm. P16–17 – Fer Gregory, Sola Solandra. P18–19 – iobard, Christian Offenberg. P20–21 – Gorodenkoff, Sebastian Kaulitzki. P22–23 – Fer Gregory, Selin Serhii. P24–25 – Plus69, Margoe Edwards, Dm_Cherry, Rizvisual. P26–27 –Fablok, A_Lesik, Marian Weyo, Melinda Nagy. P28–29 – freya–photographer, THEJAB. P30 – Ilaszlo.

Bearport Publishing Company Product Development Team
President: Jen Jenson; Director of Product Development: Spencer Brinker; Managing Editor: Allison Juda; Associate Editor: Naomi Reich; Associate Editor: Tiana Tran; Art Director: Colin O'Dea; Designer: Kim Jones; Designer: Kayla Eggert; Product Development Assistant: Owen Hamlin

Library of Congress Cataloging-in-Publication Data is available at www.loc.gov or upon request from the publisher.

ISBN: 979-8-89232-058-0 (hardcover)
ISBN: 979-8-89232-532-5 (paperback)
ISBN: 979-8-89232-191-4 (ebook)

For more information, write to Bearport Publishing, 5357 Penn Avenue South, Minneapolis, MN 55419.

CONTENTS

WHAT IS A
LIFE CYCLE?

All living things have a life cycle. Over this cycle, living things grow and change. Each step along the way is another part of their life.

Eventually, they die. Living things **reproduce** so the cycle can keep going even after they are gone. This is a normal part of living.

But what about creatures that are **paranormal**? Surely these beings would have a beginning, middle, and end to life, too. Though it might look very different from what we might expect.

People often explain away things they are scared of by telling stories. Sometimes, the stories have very strange creatures!

What would a vampire life cycle be like? Let's imagine. . . .

WHAT IS A VAMPIRE?

Vampires are popular paranormal creatures. There are stories about vampires from all over the world. Some of these stories are thousands of years old.

Most **legends** call these mysterious creatures undead. Somehow, they have escaped death. They look a lot like humans. But they are not really alive in the way humans are. Vampires do not seem to age.

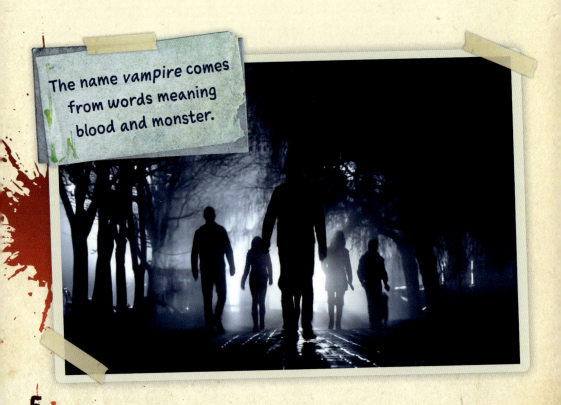

The name vampire comes from words meaning blood and monster.

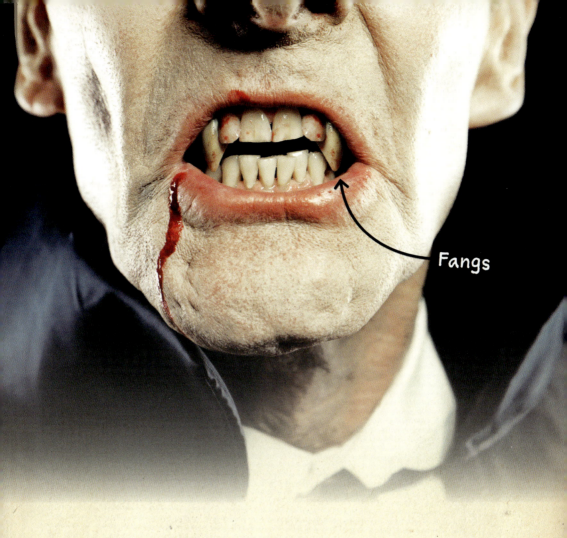

Fangs

The most important thing that sets vampires apart, however, is their fangs. In most stories, they have two sharp teeth that they use to help them drink blood.

Vampires are said to rise up at night in search of a bloody meal. In some stories, sunlight can kill them. In others, it makes their powers weaker.

BECOMING A VAMPIRE

But how does life as a vampire begin? In most stories, vampires start as living, breathing humans. Then, something happens.

Some say magic turns a human into a vampire. In some **cultures**, people believe the dead turn into vampires if a cat jumps over their bodies.

In most tales, it takes a vampire to make a vampire. A vampire's bite changes a human into the undead creature. Once the vampire sinks their teeth into the person, a **transformation** begins.

Many sicknesses spread through blood and **saliva**, so this may make some sense.

Rabies is a deadly **virus**. It can spread to humans who have been bitten by an animal sick with rabies.

THE EARLY VAMPIRE

Most sicknesses come on slowly. Becoming a vampire might as well. A person might feel the same as they do when they get the flu.

But soon, they would probably start to look like a vampire. Vampires are known for their pale skin. Maybe the transformation includes getting paler.

Sick or transforming?

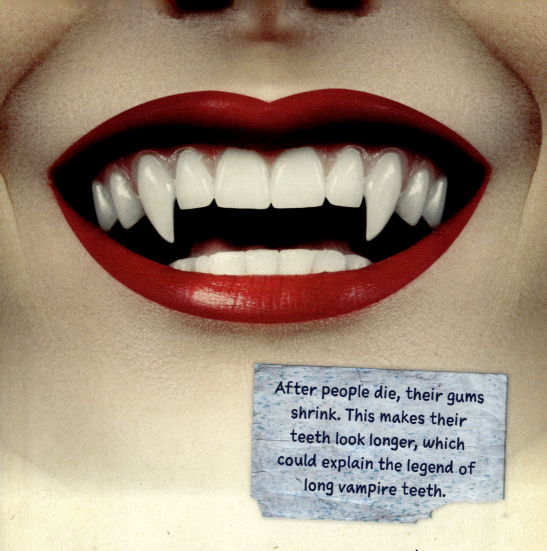

After people die, their gums shrink. This makes their teeth look longer, which could explain the legend of long vampire teeth.

Next may come the sharp vampire teeth.

Humans have pointy teeth called canines. But in vampire legends, these teeth are longer and sharper. To become a vampire, the top two canine teeth would have to change. They would need to grow and get even pointier.

THE FULLY
TRANSFORMED
VAMPIRE

Once a person turns into a vampire, they are said to begin to age very slowly. Years later, they may look the same as they did on the day they were bitten. In many stories, vampires also gain special powers.

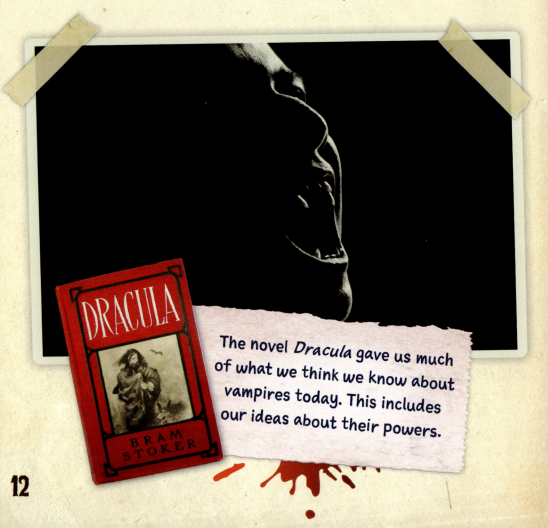

The novel *Dracula* gave us much of what we think we know about vampires today. This includes our ideas about their powers.

DRACULA

BRAM STOKER

Vampires are thought to be able to turn into bats. Many stories tell of them flying through the night in this form.

Some people say vampires are also able to **hypnotize** people. When this happens, a vampire can make a person do anything they want. Some stories say a vampire only has to look into someone's eyes to hypnotize them.

Don't look into a vampire's eyes!

DIET

In some stories, a person is a full vampire once they have grown their pointy fangs. In others, a vampire has to feed first. But there is one thing that makes up a vampire's diet. They eat blood!

A vampire uses their fangs to bite into a person. Then, they suck out the blood with their mouth.

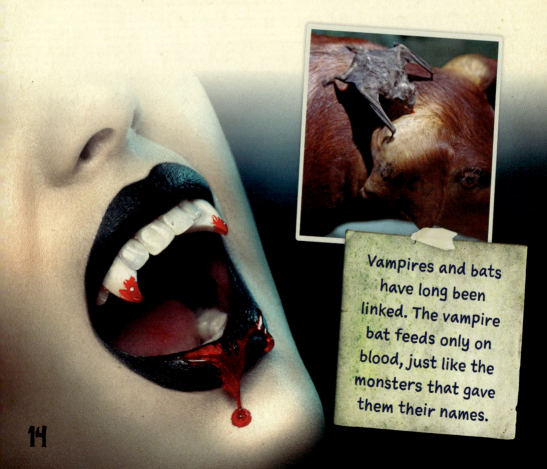

Vampires and bats have long been linked. The vampire bat feeds only on blood, just like the monsters that gave them their names.

Looking for a drink?

Like many **predators**, the search for blood would probably be an **instinct** for a vampire. This means the vampire would seek it out without thinking about what to do.

In many stories, vampires crave blood. When they don't have it, vampires get violent. This means the most dangerous kind of vampire is a thirsty one!

SHADOWY HOME

Since the sun is thought to cause them harm, vampires are said to live in shadowy places. Many stories tell of vampires living in big castles. There, they would find many dark corners.

Big castles are often mysterious to outsiders, which is probably why people think vampires would live inside.

A vampire's home?

In some cultures, people lay their dead face down in coffins. This is thought to stop them from rising from the grave.

Legends often tell of vampires sleeping during the daylight. They make their beds in coffins. While this would be sure to keep out the light, it probably started from the idea that vampires come back from death.

THE OLD VAMPIRE

Vampires are said to live hundreds or even thousands of years. Though they age very slowly, some legends say time eventually catches up. Over the years, the vampire starts to look less and less like a human and more like a bat.

All their hair falls out. Their ears become pointy, and the rest of their teeth become as sharp as their fangs.

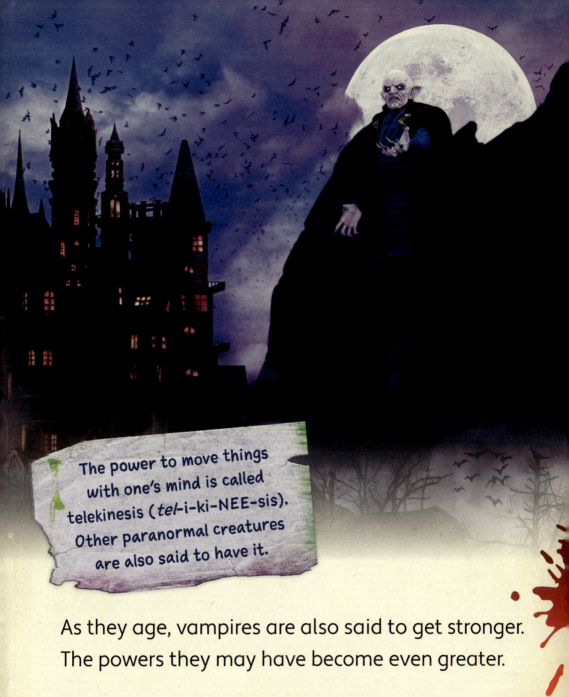

The power to move things with one's mind is called telekinesis (*tel*-i-ki-NEE-sis). Other paranormal creatures are also said to have it.

As they age, vampires are also said to get stronger. The powers they may have become even greater.

They might be able to move objects with their mind. Some stories say a strong old vampire can fly without needing to change into a bat.

MAKING MORE
BLOOD SUCKERS

While out for a bite, vampires don't think much about who they drink from. They are thought to do anything to take the blood they want.

Being able to fly may help them get where they want to go quickly. Hypnotizing someone could make it easy to convince a person to become a meal.

Old legends don't talk much about where a vampire bites. But today's tales usually say they drink from the neck. This makes some sense. We need a lot of blood for our brains to work. It travels there through the neck.

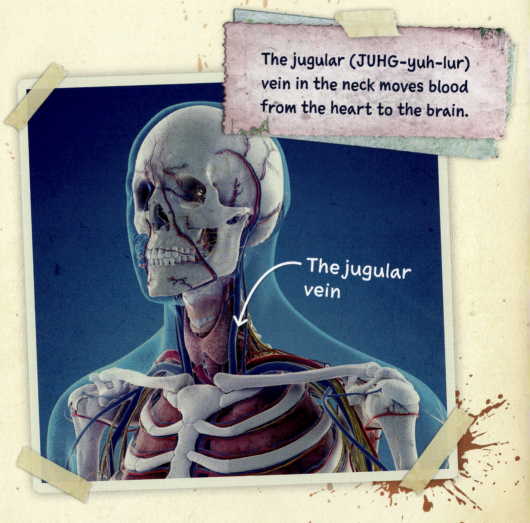

The jugular (JUHG-yuh-lur) vein in the neck moves blood from the heart to the brain.

The jugular vein

If a victim isn't sucked dry, they will turn into a vampire themself. And the cycle continues. . . .

TYPES OF VAMPIRES

Many stories of vampires are similar. But there are a few that tell of different kinds of vampires.

PSYCHIC VAMPIRES

Psychic vampires do not suck blood. They are hungry for another part of a person . . . their mind!

It is said that these vampires just need to get close to a person to drain their thoughts.

REVENANTS

Revenants drink blood, but it is not the only thing they want.

These creatures are out for **revenge**. Revenants climb out of their graves to hunt people who upset them during their lives.

The name for these vampires comes from a French word meaning to return.

SPOTTING A VAMPIRE

If vampires look a lot like humans, how could you spot one? There are some things you could watch out for.

EYES

Where are they looking? If someone can't keep their eyes off your neck, they may be planning their next bite!

AVOIDS SUNLIGHT

If the sun harms vampires, they would probably avoid it. Keep an eye on anyone staying in the dark.

MIRRORS

Many stories say vampires do not have a **reflection**. When they look in a mirror, there is nothing there. If you think someone wants to suck your blood, check to see if they have a reflection.

In some stories, vampires don't have a shadow, either.

Blood?

RED DRINKS

Watch out for anyone taking a sip of something red. Who knows what could be in their glass. . . .

HOW TO DEAL WITH A
VAMPIRE

If you were to ever find a vampire, don't panic!
The stories also tell of ways to protect yourself.

GARLIC

Legends say vampires
hate garlic. This might
be because it has a very
strong flavor. Whatever the
reason, keep a bulb around.

Vampires
stay away!

UNWELCOME GUESTS

Many stories say vampires cannot enter a place
unless they are invited inside. Don't let strangers in!

Stories say that driving a
wooden stake into a vampire's
heart will kill it.

LIGHT

If the sun makes a vampire weaker, finding light is a great way to stay safe. Keep the curtains open. If you can, stay outside during the day!

ROSES

Some stories say that wild roses can keep vampires away. The flowers were put on the coffins of people thought to be vampires to trap them inside.

LIFE CYCLE OF A VAMPIRE

So, what might the life cycle of a vampire look like? It would start with one bite. If the person survived being a living blood bag, they would start to turn into a vampire.

They would become pale. Their teeth would grow into deadly fangs. And they would become thirsty for blood.

Some vampires may start to feel special powers that help them hunt down a meal.

Slowly, as a vampire gets older, it may start to look uglier. It may also get more powerful.

Along the way, the vampire would create even more monsters like itself. According to stories, they would go on living for hundreds or thousands of years.

Most living things don't even reach 100. However, there is a clam known to live to be more than 500 years old.

BEWARE THE PARANORMAL!

There are stories around the world of all sorts of paranormal creatures. If you want to learn more, be very careful. . . .

Vampires may be dangerous, but what if there is something even worse creeping around in the dark? How would their scary life cycle begin, continue, and end?

GLOSSARY

cultures the customs and traditions shared by groups of people

hypnotize to control another person's mind by putting them into a trance

instinct things animals do or know naturally, without having to learn

legends stories that are handed down from the past

paranormal things that are not able to be explained by science

predators animals that hunt and kill other animals for food

reflection the image of something on a shiny surface

reproduce to make more of a living thing

revenge punishment for something that has been done

saliva the liquid in the mouths of humans and other animals

transformation an act, process, or example of changing into something else

virus a tiny thing that causes diseases in people and other animals

INDEX

READ MORE

Gleason, Carrie. *Guide to Vampires (Cryptid Guides: Creatures of Folklore).* New York: Crabtree Publishing, 2023.

Redshaw, Hermione. *The Invasion of the Vampires (Supernatural Survivor).* Minneapolis: Bearport Publishing Company, 2023.

LEARN MORE ONLINE

1. Go to **www.factsurfer.com** or scan the QR code below.

2. Enter **"Vampire Life Cycle"** into the search box.

3. Click on the cover of this book to see a list of websites.